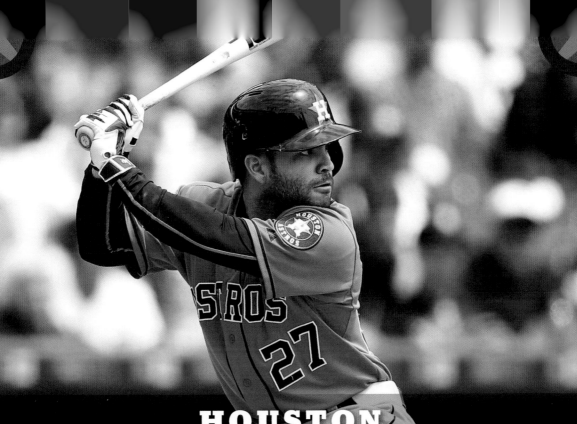

HOUSTON
ASTROS
STARS, STATS, HISTORY, AND MORE!

BY CONOR BUCKLEY

The Child's World®
childsworld.com

Published by The Child's World®
1980 Lookout Drive • Mankato, MN 56003-1705
800-599-READ • www.childsworld.com

ISBN 9781503828247
LCCN 2018944837

Printed in the United States of America
PAO2392

Photo Credits:
Cover: Joe Robbins (2).
Interior: AP Images: Richard Carson/Houston Chronicle
8, Aaron M. Sprecher 14, Keith Krakocic 19; Newscom:
Kevin Dietsch/UPI 4, Jim Ruyman/UPI 17, Leslie Plaza
Johnson/Icon SW 20, Rich Kane/Icon SMI 23, Nick
Wosika/Icon SMI 27, Richard C. Lewis/Icon SMI 29; Joe
Robbins: 7, 11, 24, ; Wikimedia: Brian Reading 12.

About the Author
Conor Buckley is a lifelong baseball fan now studying for a career in esports. His books in this series are his first published works.

On the Cover
Main photo: All-Star José Altuve
Inset: Hall of Fame pitcher
Nolan Ryan

CONTENTS

GO, ASTROS!

Houston has gone from worst to first. The Astros were pretty bad for several seasons. Then they started winning. Houston fans were thrilled when the team brought home the 2017 **World Series** title! What's next for this superstar team? Let's meet the Houston Astros!

 Time to celebrate! A trio of Astros jump for joy after a win in 2018.

WHO ARE THE ASTROS?

Houston plays in the American League (AL). That group is part of Major League Baseball (MLB). MLB also includes the National League (NL). There are 30 teams in MLB. The winner of the AL plays the winner of the NL in the World Series. From 1962 to 2012, Houston played in the NL!

Justin Verlander is the top pitcher on the Astros. ➤

WHERE THEY CAME FROM

The Astros started in 1962. In their first three seasons, the team was called the Colt .45s. In 1965, the team moved into a brand-new stadium, the Houston Astrodome. The stadium was named for American astronauts. Houston was the center of the U.S. space program. Before they moved to the new stadium, the team changed its name to the Astros.

◆ *Fireworks indoors? Yes, the old Houston Astrodome was that big!*

WHO THEY PLAY

The Astros play 162 games in a season. That's a lot of baseball! They play most of their games against other AL teams. The Astros are part of the AL West Division. The other AL West teams are the Los Angeles Angels, the Oakland Athletics, the Seattle Mariners, and the Texas Rangers. Houston also plays NL teams.

Dallas Keuchel is famous for his beard . . . and his great pitching. ➤

WHERE THEY PLAY

Minute Maid Park in Houston is named for an orange juice company. Minute Maid paid the Astros for the right to name the stadium. The park was built near Union Station. Because of that, the stadium builders included a small train. The train runs along the outfield wall when the Astros hit a homer. The roof in Minute Maid Park can open and close. This helps protect fans and players from the Texas heat.

◄ *This mini-train chugs around the walls of Minute Maid Park.*

THE BASEBALL FIELD

FOUL LINE ↘

THIRD BASE ➤

DUGOUT ▼

PITCHER'S MOUND ▲

ON-DECK CIRCLE ↘

HOME PLATE ▲

COACH'S BOX ▲

THE INTERNATIONAL BROTHERHOOD OF ELECTRICAL WORKERS LOCAL 716

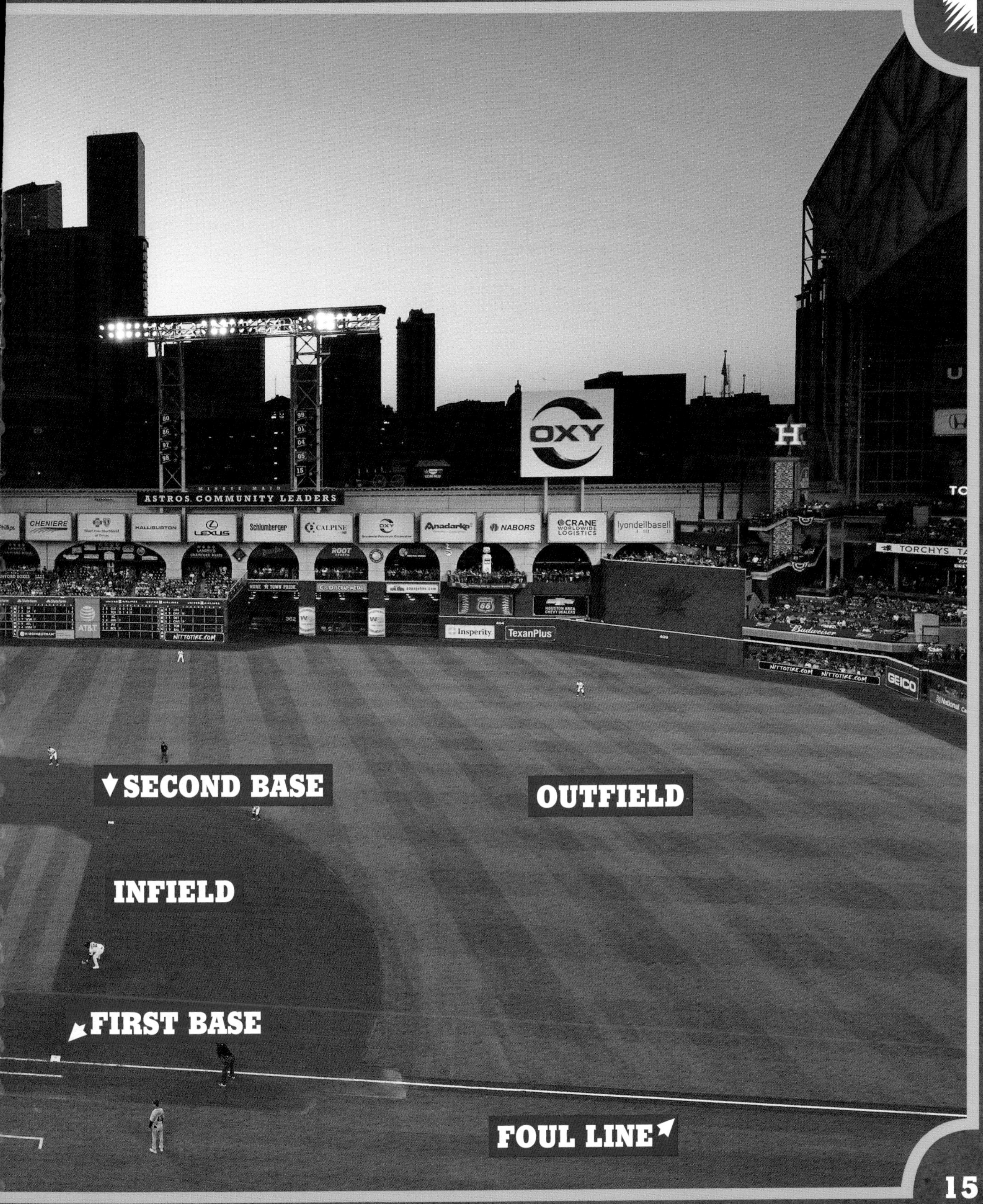

OXY

ASTROS. COMMUNITY LEADERS

▼SECOND BASE

OUTFIELD

INFIELD

◄FIRST BASE

FOUL LINE◄

BIG DAYS

The Astros are one of the newest teams in the AL. Here are some of their best performances.

1980—The Astros won their first division title. They lost in the **playoffs** to the Phillies, but it was a great season in Houston!

2005—The Astros earned their first league championship!

2017—Houston won its first World Series! The team's fans were thrilled! The Astros beat the Los Angeles Dodgers in an exciting series.

Justin Verlander and José Altuve proudly hold ➤
the World Series championship trophy.

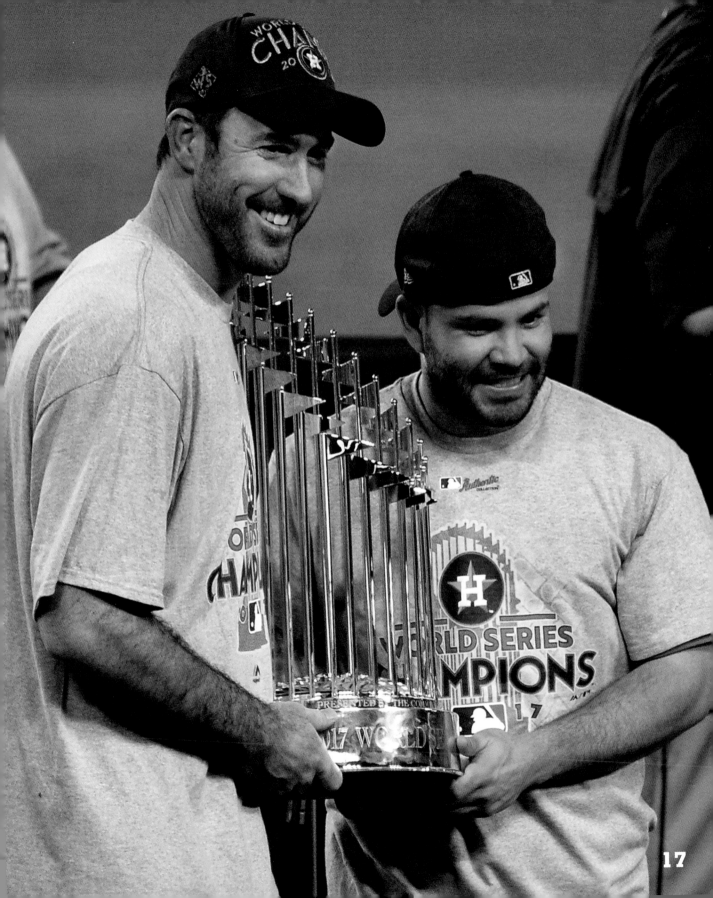

TOUGH DAYS

Here's a look back at some games and seasons Astros fans might want to forget!

1971—Houston **traded** second baseman Joe Morgan to the Cincinnati Reds. Oops. Morgan helped the Reds win two World Series and he was named the NL **MVP** twice!

1989—In a game against the Reds, the Astros got off to a really bad start. They gave up 14 runs in the first inning! They ended up losing 18-2.

2013—The Astros lost 111 games this season. That was the most in team history. Four years later, they were World Series champs!

Another error! That's how it went for the Astros in 2013! ➤

MEET THE FANS!

Astros fans are patient. They are *very* patient. From 2011 to 2013, Houston lost more than 300 games! The team was slowly building up a great roster. It was hard to wait and watch all that losing. The fans got their reward when Houston won the World Series in 2017. Helping them cheer is the team's fuzzy green **mascot**, Orbit.

◀ *Orbit is an alien, thanks to Houston's space connections.*

HEROES THEN

The most famous players in Astros history are the "Killer Bs." Three players with "B" last names helped Houston win again and again. Craig Biggio played second base. He was a great hitter and stole lots of bases. Lance Berkman played outfield. He was a big slugger, with five seasons of 30 or more homers. The best Astros player ever was probably Jeff Bagwell. The powerful first baseman hit more than 400 homers. He was named to the **Hall of Fame** in 2017.

Bagwell used a very wide batting style, but it worked! ➤

HEROES NOW

José Altuve is pretty short, but he's powerful. The second baseman led the team to its 2017 World Series win. He's a three-time AL batting champ. George Springer has smacked many big homers for the Astros. Alex Bregman plays infield and has lots of **clutch** hits. Justin Verlander is a top pitcher. He joined Houston in 2017 and helped them win it all. Strikeout pitcher Gerrit Cole joined the team in 2018.

◀ Altuve uses his speed to score another run for the Astros.

GEARING UP

Baseball players wear team uniforms. On defense, they wear leather gloves to catch the ball. As batters, they wear hard helmets. This protects them from pitches. Batters hit the ball with long wood bats. Each player chooses his own size of bat. Catchers have the toughest job. They wear a lot of protection.

THE BASEBALL

The outside of the Major League baseball is made from cow leather. Two leather pieces shaped like 8s are stitched together. There are 108 stitches of red thread. These stitches help players grip the ball. Inside, the ball has a small center of cork and rubber. Hundreds of feet of yarn are tightly wound around this center.

◄ **CATCHER'S MASK AND HELMET**

◄ **CHEST PROTECTOR**

◄ **WRIST BANDS**

▲ **CATCHER'S MITT**

▲ **SHIN GUARDS**

CATCHER'S GEAR

TEAM STATS

ere are some of the all-time career records for the Houston Astros. All of these stats are through the 2018 regular season.

HOME RUNS

Jeff Bagwell	449
Lance Berkman	326

RBI

Jeff Bagwell	1,529
Craig Biggio	1,175

BATTING AVERAGE

Moises Alou	.331
José Altuve	.316

STRIKEOUTS

Nolan Ryan	1,866
Roy Oswalt	1,593

WINS

Joe Niekro	144
Roy Oswalt	143

SAVES

Billy Wagner	225
Dave Smith	199

Craig Biggio was a great hitter and base-stealer. ➤

STOLEN BASES

Cesar Cedeno	487
Craig Biggio	414

GLOSSARY

clutch (KLUTCH) coming through when a team needs a player most

Hall of Fame (HALL UV FAYM) a building in Cooperstown, New York, that honors baseball's greatest players

mascot (MASS-cot) costumed character who helps fans cheer

MVP stands for Most Valuable Player, an award given to the top player in each league

playoffs (PLAY-offs) after the regular schedule, the games played to determine who goes to the World Series

traded (TRAY-ded) swapped with a player from another team

World Series (WURLD SEE-reez) the annual championship of Major League Baseball

FIND OUT MORE

IN THE LIBRARY

Aretha, David. *José Altuve: Champion Baseball Star*. New York, NY: Enslow, 2017.

Connery-Boyd, Peg. *Houston Astros: The Big Book of Baseball Activities*. Chicago, IL: Sourcebooks Jabberwocky, 2016.

Sports Illustrated Kids (editors). *The Big Book of Who: Baseball*. New York, NY: Sports Illustrated Kids, 2017.

ON THE WEB

Visit our website for links about the Houston Astros: **childsworld.com/links**

Note to Parents, Teachers, and Librarians: We routinely verify our Web links to make sure they are safe and active sites. So encourage your readers to check them out!

INDEX